ENCHANTED EARTH

LOM
ART

Illustrated by

Melpomeni
Chatzipanagiotou

This book was
coloured by

. . . .

Edited by Jocelyn Norbury
Cover design by Angie Allison

First published in Great Britain in 2023 by LOM ART,
an imprint of Michael O'Mara Books Limited,
9 Lion Yard, Tremadoc Road, London SW4 7NQ

W www.mombooks.com/lom
f Michael O'Mara Books
🐦 @OMaraBooks
📷 @lomart.books

A CIP catalogue record for this book is available from the British Library.

ISBN: 978-1-912785-80-3

1 3 5 7 9 10 8 6 4 2

This book was printed in China.

FSC
www.fsc.org

MIX
Paper | Supporting
responsible forestry
FSC® C010256

Enter an enchanted world

Relax and colour this collection of
striking and original illustrations that
explore worlds within worlds.

Discover a secret riverside scene under a
canopy of mushrooms, the head of a woman
formed from flowers and an owl carrying
rugged mountains on its wings.

The images magically and inventively
combine elements from natural
and fantasy worlds.

These spellbinding scenes
are waiting to be brought
to life with colour.

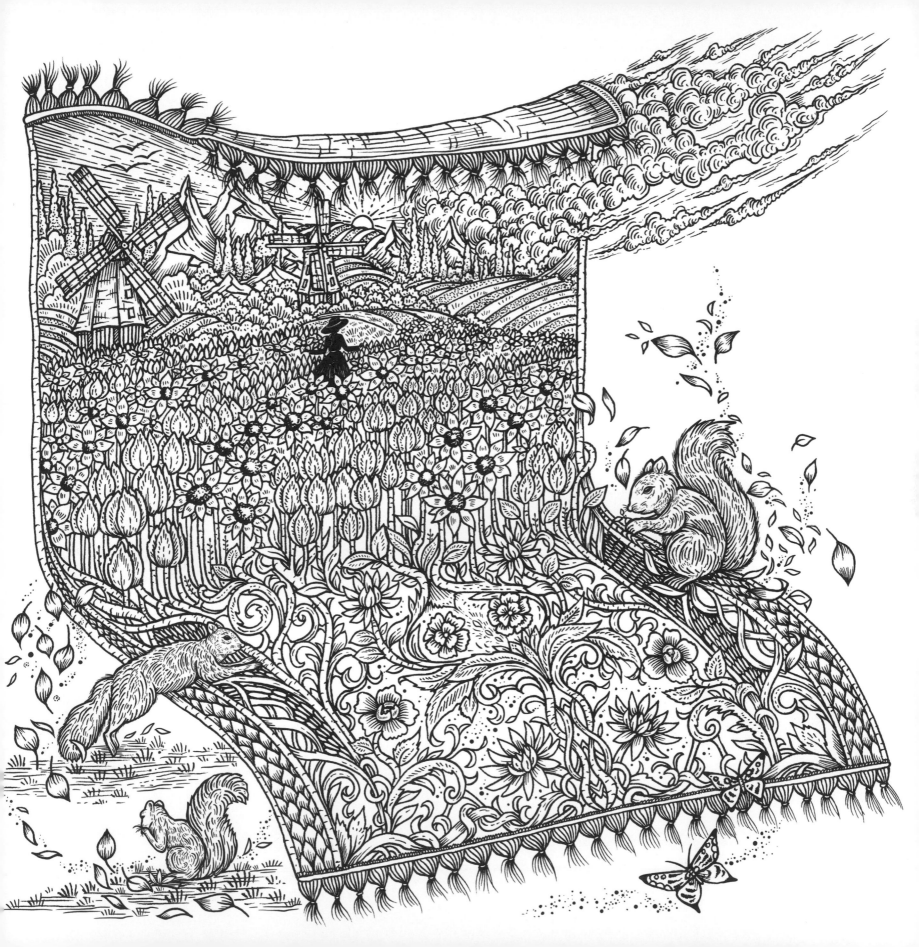

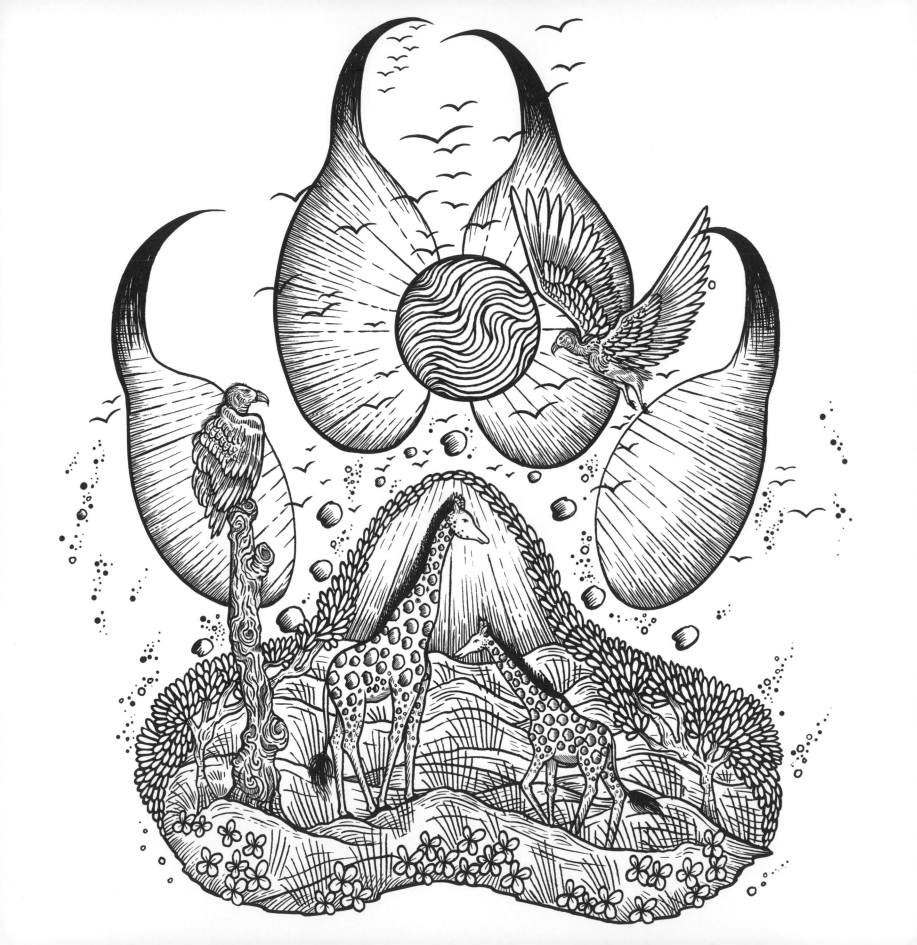

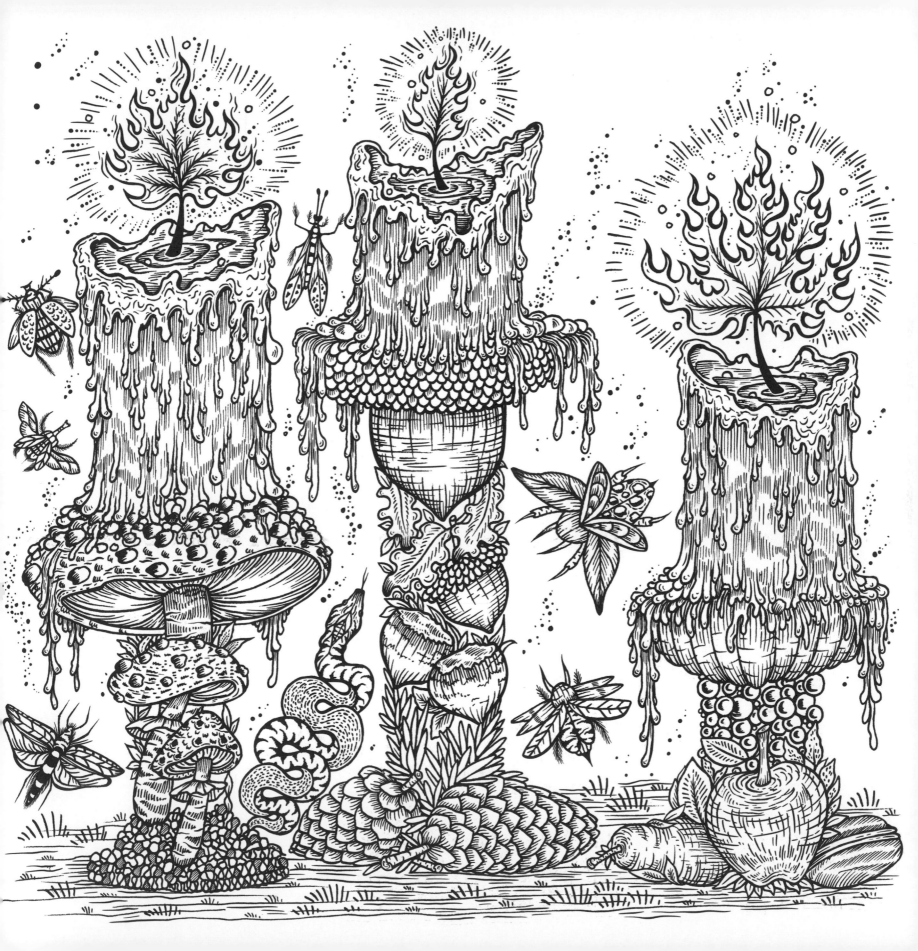